Why Don't They Follow Me?
12 Easy Lessons to Boost Your Leadership Skills

Cover Design by Kiwi Creative, KiwiCreative.com

Copyright © 2009, 2016 by Pacelli Publishing
9905 Lake Washington Blvd. NE, #D-103
Bellevue WA 98004
PacelliPublishing.com

ISBN-10: 1-933750-18-9
ISBN-13: 978-1-933750-18-7

For ML, Boop, and GM

LEADERSHIP LESSONS

Class is in Session!.. 9

Humor–Credibility=Doofus.................................13

Knowledge–Listening=Arrogance...........................21

Action–Integrity=Distrust.............................29

Activity–Focus=Randomness.................................35

Wisdom–Experience=Theory...............................43

Ability–Effort=Inaction.............................51

Leadership–Inspiration=Administration 57

Charisma–Conviction=Crooked Politician 65

Courage–Predictability=Recklessness..................71

Smarts–Direction=Absent Minded Professor.....77

Communication–Candor=Storyteller....................83

Decisiveness–Empathy=Ruthlessness..................89

Get Your Cap and Gown!................................95

Why Don't They Follow Me?

Let's do a little exercise.

Think about the term "leader" and associate it with either a public figure or a person you know. Who did you conjure up? Maybe it was a governmental head of state; or maybe a military general; or possibly a corporate executive; or perhaps a professional sports figure. It's true that these high-profile positions carry great responsibility and are charged with leading important causes. The truth is, though, that virtually any situation where a person has to assemble, organize, guide, and inspire a group of people to get something done is using the same leadership muscles that high-profile leaders need to use. Think about the job of a PTA president (of which my wife was for a number of years); she needs to get things done using a volunteer force of parents who sometimes deliver but many times don't. Her job as a leader is in many ways more difficult than that of a corporate executive or military general in that there is no personal consequence for not following the leader. If one of her PTA board members doesn't follow through there is no firing or being "thrown in the brink" awaiting the board member. She has to get the board to *want* to follow her to get things done.

It is for leaders like the PTA president that I wrote **Why Don't They Follow Me?**

As I look back at my biggest screw-ups in over 30 years as a leader (and I've had a ton of them!) they weren't because of a complex business problem or a deep technical issue. They were because I didn't fully grasp that a leader's positive actions can easily be outweighed by his negative actions. Let's take lesson #1, Humor – Credibility = Doofus as an example. Humor can be a very positive attribute of any leader and is one that shows the human-ness of the leader. The use of humor becomes a problem when the leader hasn't previously established credibility with his team. So, while the leader has established that he has a funny side, his team will be reluctant to follow him because he hasn't proven himself worthy of being followed. It is the inter-relationship of these key leadership attributes and how bad attributes outweigh good which **Why Don't They Follow Me?** focuses upon.

Why Don't They Follow Me? presents must-need leadership attributes in an easy-to-understand format that both new and experienced leaders will quickly grasp and apply. Perhaps you lead a team in your daily job; or own a small business; or lead a small non-profit organization. Quite frankly, it just doesn't matter when it comes to these principles; if you want and need people to follow your leadership, this book is for you.

Each leadership lesson is presented in a consistent format using icons to help you quickly navigate the content and efficiently refer back to points when you need them.

 Learning the lesson - This section focuses on a definition of the principle and some root causes as to why leaders fail at the principle.

 Adding it up - This section focuses on at least three helpful tips which you as a leader can use to improve your leadership skills.

 Graduating with honors - This section gives you a summary of the leadership lesson and gives final tips on how to avoid screw-ups of your own.

My hope is that you are able to quickly grasp the 12 leadership principles, determine which of the principles are problem areas for you, and take away just a couple of nuggets to help you put new tools in your leadership toolbox and improve your skills as a leader.

To your leadership journey -

Lonnie Pacelli

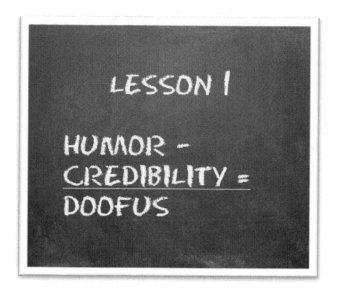

Ed was just appointed team leader in a public works organization of the federal government. In preparing for his first meeting with his new team, Ed thought long and hard about some of his prior managers' leadership styles. One characteristic he particularly admired in several of his managers was the ability to connect with the team through humor. He decided on a strategy that would help the team accept him as a leader—he would show his human side and use humor to connect with them.

Ed had his first meeting with the team and was very satisfied with the results. The team seemed to really like him. The meeting was filled with laughter and both the team and Ed seemed to really be enjoying themselves.   Ed was very happy and believed things were getting off to a great start.

With each passing meeting, though, there seemed to be a growing concern among the team. While Ed seemed to connect with the team, he didn't see the cooperation on getting things done as he had hoped. There were also a couple of team members who asked for permission to interview for positions outside of the group.   Ed was growing concerned over the trend and asked Betty, one of the team members, what she thought was the problem. Betty's counsel hit Ed right between the eyes: "Ed, you're a great guy and people really like you, but I just don't know if you've got what it takes to lead this group. The team is concerned which makes me concerned." While Ed's focus on using humor to connect with the team was great, he didn't take the time to establish the necessary credibility with them.

Learning the Lesson:
Any one of us can think about an influential figure we've had in our lives, whether a parent, boss, or religious leader, who used humor to build camaraderie and inspire people. Leaders who have a sense of humor motivate those around him to want to participate in the journey. The problem arises, though, when a leader tries to connect with a team of people prior to establishing himself as *worthy* of being

followed. If a leader fails to establish his worthiness by gaining credibility with the team, the team may only stick with the leader when things are going well and there are no problems on the horizon. The moment that problems start cropping up, team members will be more apt to defect because they won't have faith in the leader to navigate the storm. *Credibility breeds acceptance, humor fosters inspiration.*

So why is the failure to establish credibility such a massive issue? Here are the biggies:

- **Team members need to trust that the leader can get from origin to destination** – Being a leader means knowing the plan and leading the team down the field. The leader not only needs to know the plan and how to execute, she needs to communicate the plan to the team and ensure the team understands and believes in the plan.

- **Team members need to feel secure that the leader will navigate well through stormy issues** – Think of an airline flight you've been on where some unexpected turbulence hit. While the plane is rocking and rolling, the pilot speaks to the passengers with incredible calmness and control. His job is to make you feel that things are well in hand. Imagine if turbulence hit and you heard the pilot say "We've got problems and I'm not sure what to do!" I'd be heading to the cockpit to fly the bird myself (and I can barely fly a kite never mind a plane!) Having credibility with the team gives the team greater security that the leader will get them through sticky issues.

- **Use of humor by a credibility-starved leader will exacerbate the credibility issue** – When leaders continually use humor as a means to connect with a team without establishing credibility up-front, the use of humor itself becomes a credibility inhibitor. Teams will tend to see the use of humor as the leader trying to "cover up" the fact that he may not know what he is doing. Thus, each time the credibility-starved leader cracks a joke, he is actually reinforcing this lack of credibility issue with the team. Rather than seizing the opportunity to gain credibility, the leader uses it to brush up on his lounge act.

Adding it up:
Appropriate use of humor is a great means to inspire a team to perform, so long as the credibility has already been established. Use the following tips to help you get over the credibility hump:

- **Start with listening** – Gaining credibility doesn't mean you have all the answers before you understand the questions. In fact, not taking the time to listen can actually hurt your credibility campaign and brand you as arrogant (we'll talk more about this in lesson #2). Demonstrating a clear understanding of team concerns and issues is a great credibility builder in that the team learns to trust you as a leader.

- **Use humor sparingly up front** – The team first and foremost wants to know why they should be following you. Use those initial opportunities with the team to connect through understanding the issues they are facing and gaining an understanding of the most important things for you as a leader to focus on. As you build the credibility, feel free to introduce more humor to move the team from *accepting* you to being *inspired* to follow you.

- **Don't be so gun-shy of using humor that you are viewed as a stick-in-the-mud** – Being cautious about using humor shouldn't give you a reputation as stern, mean, or stoic. By all means, be pleasant, approachable, and engaged in your interaction. The team will find it easier to talk to you and will get a more comfortable feeling that you understand their problems.

- **Use a bit of self-deprecating humor** – I use this technique a lot particularly when I am doing presentations. I will frequently tell of a situation where I did something really foolish or where I publicly embarrassed myself in front of a group of people. This demonstrates that you're secure enough with your own abilities to share them with other people. It also shows that you are able to laugh at *yourself* and not take yourself too seriously. One note of caution here: don't be self-deprecating to a point that the team sees you as having a self-esteem issue.

- **Avoid humor which tarnishes the credibility of others** – Using humor which trashes other people or competitors creates problems in a couple of ways for you as a leader. The first has to do with the trustworthiness of the leader. While team members may see destructive jokes as funny, they can develop a viewpoint of "so what does this person say about *me* when I'm not in the room?" The second has to do with the questionability of your motivations. When you trash talk others for a laugh, you can be viewed as attempting to build your credibility at the expense of someone else through your own insight and wit. For credibility to be well entrenched in the team it needs to be absolute, not relative. Otherwise, you're only demonstrating that you are worthy to lead a team until someone better or smarter comes along. Not a good foundation to establish credibility.

 Graduating with honors:
Look, none of us wants to follow a leader with all the personality of cottage cheese. Having a leader who is able to share an occasional joke and laugh with a team is huge in moving a team from *acceptance* to

inspiration. Just ensure that you as a leader take the first step to establish credibility with the team and garner their trust in you before you get too liberal with the funny stuff.

Why Don't They Follow Me?

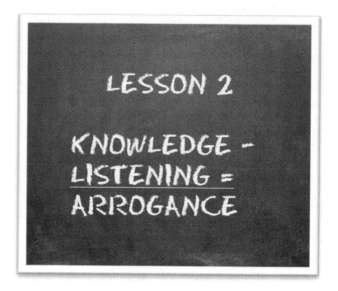

R on was a newly appointed leader of a large nonprofit organization. He was widely regarded as a foremost authority in his field. He held advanced degrees from two prestigious universities and a number of awards for his research. He had experience in both for-profit and nonprofit organizations and clearly demonstrated his command of his subject matter. Ron seemed to be the perfect fit for the organization.

As Ron was preparing to join the organization, he began developing his game plan for what he would focus on first. He had extensively researched the organization and come up with some very clear ideas about what he wanted to change. On his first day, Ron introduced himself to his staff and expressed to each of them how excited he was to have the job. He held a staff meeting later that day to reiterate his excitement. They were thrilled to have such a renowned authority leading the organization.

Over the first couple of weeks, Ron introduced a total of ten ideas to his staff which he wanted to get started on right away. The staff thought the ideas were very innovative and held great promise for the organization, but thought Ron was giving them too much work and wanted him to focus on just a couple of the ideas first. Ron was pretty put off by the staff's feedback and continued to press to complete the work on all ten of the ideas at once. As Ron continued to press the staff, they grew increasingly uncomfortable with the amount of work being thrust upon them and his delivery expectations. The pressure became too much for a number of the staff members which led them to resign from the organization. The remaining staff members went to the organization's board of directors and complained about Ron's sky-high expectations and unwillingness to listen to the staff's input. The board listened to the staff members and began observing Ron's leadership style. Over a three-month period, Ron's attitude of, "I know what's best more than you do," came through in a number of situations. Despite his knowledge of the subject matter, the board decided to remove Ron from his leadership position because he refused to listen to viewpoints which differed from his own.

 Learning the Lesson:
A leader could have enough experience, knowledge and industry accolades to fill a grain elevator. He could know how to work his or her way out of the most difficult of situations. The problem arises when a leader becomes so self-confident and self-important that he doesn't view his team's viewpoints as credible when compared to his own. When this self-sufficiency sets in, the leader becomes increasingly resistant to listen to the team simply because others don't measure up in his mind. The natural consequence is that the team finds it difficult to willingly follow the leader. Despite all of the leader's strengths, he will be more associated with **arrogance** than **knowledge**.

So why all the hubbub? If the leader has the capability to deliver results, so what if he doesn't listen to the team? It's a big problem for a few reasons:

- **Team members inherently want to be heard** – Being part of a well-oiled team means that each team member deserves an opportunity to express concerns, contribute ideas, and help set direction. Giving team members a platform to express themselves boosts their self-esteem and confidence, particularly when they are working with a high-profile leader.

- **Team members execute better when they feel ownership of the direction** – Team members need to know they can provide input into the direction the team is taking and shape how things are accomplished. Providing an opportunity for a team member to put a thumbprint on direction will create a sense of ownership and personal accountability.

- **Team members are more likely to take on a defeatist attitude when not listened to** – When a leader doesn't listen to his team, the team will do what the leader wants, but will give up if things start going south. Rather than the team redoubling its efforts to make things work, the members are more apt to take on an "I told you so" attitude and mentally accept defeat. Sure, the team may still go through the motions, but the passion and desire to execute will be diminished.

As a leader, it's also easy to take listening to an extreme. There are two key dangers leaders need to be cognizant of when listening to the team:

- **The leader chronically reopens issues whenever a team member expresses a concern** – Permitting a team to chronically reopen issues whenever a team member expresses a concern not only dilutes the focus of a team, but will frustrate other team members. When resolving issues, there is a time to listen, a time to decide, a time to act, and a time to evaluate. Inappropriately reopening issues in the spirit of listening will slow the team down.

- **The leader doesn't apply his or her own knowledge** – A leader needs to listen, but also needs to apply his own knowledge before taking action. When a leader responds to a team member concern without validating it against his point of view, the team loses the benefit of the leader's experience and knowledge. Just as important, the team is likely to lose confidence in the leader if he only responds to the "squeaky wheels" on the team.

Adding it up:
To strike the right listening balance and avoid being labeled as arrogant, consider the following:

- **Give plenty of time for team discussion** – When discussing direction or evaluating solution alternatives, give the team plenty of time to talk through options, express opinions, or come up with a better idea. With little exception, every time I've done this with my team the solution was made better as a result.

- **Do some impromptu discussions** – Don't be afraid to do an occasional drop-in on a team member to chat and ask her what she thinks about a particular topic or issue. Aside from getting some great ideas, you'll also build relationships with team members. Just make sure you don't drop in on the same one or two people all the time or they will be labeled as your "favorites."

- **Practice restating** – To hone your listening skills, focus on restating a key point that a team member is expressing. To help you remember and digest the restatement, try putting the key point in your own words then get confirmation from the team member that you understood her point. Just don't become a parrot and repeat phrases ad nauseum, or you'll come across as insincere.

- **Openly praise those who speak up** – Encourage team members to voice their viewpoints, challenge ideas, and raise concerns. Once team members understand that you promote listening to their thoughts, they will feel more open about bringing out ideas and be more willing to stand by you and deliver.

- **Explain the reasons when you choose not to take action** – Listening to a team member doesn't mean you will always do what is suggested. What is important, though, is to clearly explain your action or inaction to your team. "Because I said so" never worked when we were children and definitely doesn't work as adults. Let the team in on your thinking; they may not be thrilled with the answer but at least they will understand the rationale behind the answer and will respect your point of view.

Graduating with honors:
A key aspect of being a leader means balancing your knowledge with the knowledge of others through active, sincere listening. Let your team know you are very open to hearing their viewpoints and want to learn from them. Just make sure you balance listening with focusing on the task, and apply your own experience and knowledge to the situation.

Why Don't They Follow Me?

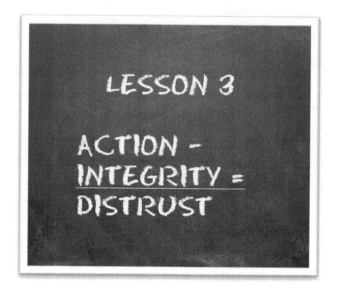

ndrew was your prototypical type-A personality. He was a very hard driver who wasn't afraid to take on hard tasks, work until midnight, and produce a finished product ahead of schedule. Andrew took great pride in his ability to deliver results and expected to be well-rewarded for his work.

The team leader in Andrew's organization was transferred to another organization and Barb, the organization's director, took on the task to find a new team leader. Andrew was very excited to interview for the position and felt that with his history of delivering results he was a shoo-in for the job. Andrew went through the interview process along with two other candidates. After the interviews were complete, Barb announced Alice, one of Andrew's peers, as the new team leader. Andrew's heart sank at the news and he couldn't believe that Alice was chosen over him given his track record.

After a few days passed, Andrew asked Barb if they could grab a cup of coffee and talk about Barb's decision to hire Alice over Andrew. Barb agreed and the two went out for coffee. "Barb, I just don't understand why I wasn't chosen for the position," Andrew said. "I deliver better than anyone on the team and am your top performer; why didn't I get the job?" "I'm glad you asked, Andrew," Barb started. "You work incredibly hard and make a tremendous effort, but I'm not comfortable that you can lead a team effectively yet. You appear to take a 'What's best for Andrew' approach to your work and I don't feel comfortable that you will consistently lead with the interests of the organization in mind. The motivations under which you operate cause other team members to question your integrity, which is a fundamental requirement for any leader, regardless of how action-oriented he or she is. You need to work on this issue before you're entrusted with a team, Andrew; I hope you're able to address this and become a strong leader in the future." Andrew couldn't help but do some serious introspection on his motives and made a commitment to address any question about his integrity.

Learning the Lesson:

Action-oriented leaders are a dream-come-true for project teams, stake-holders, and customers. Those mover and shaker leaders don't take "no" for an answer lightly, are able to get others to execute quickly, and have the capability to deliver results effectively. While having the ability to take action is a crucial characteristic of an effective leader, not all actions are done for the greater good of the team or for the organization as a whole. Actions which emanate from a leader who has a tarnished integrity will invariably result in team members, stakeholders, and customers questioning the motives of the leader and will create distrust between the leader and the team. Rather than others viewing the leader's actions as "What's good for the *organization*," the leader's actions may be viewed as "What's good for the *leader*."

Having questionable integrity dampens effective leadership in the following ways:

- **Team members may follow the leader, but will do so with reservation** – The team may see the virtues in following a leader's direction, but when that leader has questionable integrity, they will follow willingly only if they are comfortable with the leader's motivations. If there is any feeling that the leader is operating with less than forthright integrity, the team's willingness to follow will be hampered.

- **Team members will be on the watch for "about faces"** – Leaders with questionable integrity tend to operate more like a sailboat adrift on the open seas. The leader will tend to sail in whichever direction the political winds are blowing. As the leader changes direction, the team is likely to become frustrated due to wasted time and effort.

- **Team members will be less likely to "go the extra mile" for the leader** – When team members question a leader's integrity, they'll do what is asked and will work to accomplish an objective, but giving that extra bit for the leader to get a task done is going to be more difficult for team members to do. Team members who are loyal to a leader with high integrity will put their all into producing a high-quality result. Team members who work for a leader with questionable integrity will do only what's necessary to finish the task.

Adding it up:
So, OK, by now you probably get the point that action-oriented leaders with questionable integrity won't garner the same level of trust and respect that a high-integrity leader will command. Here are a few things to consider which will help you remove the *question* from *questionable* integrity and get the most out of your action:

- **Do what you say, say what you do** – It's simple; actions need to follow words. When you say something but do something different, the likelihood that someone will believe you the next time is reduced. Make sure your words and actions sync up.

- **Be organization- or team-first in your thoughts and actions** – Clearly understand and articulate the best thing for your organization or team, then ensure your actions align with those needs. It's rare that a leader personally loses out when he has considered the best interests of the organization or team more important than his own. Know what the objectives are for the organization or team and set sail for those objectives.

- **Use a coach to check your actions** – Ask a colleague who is direct and trustworthy to tell you when your actions aren't aligning with your words or when you appear to be putting your personal motivations over those of the organization or team. This can be a mentor, a coworker, or even one of your team members. Just make sure not to "shoot the messenger" if you hear something you don't like.

- **Clearly explain how a particular decision you've made aligns with the needs of the organization or team** – Make it a point to clearly explain your decision-making thought process and how the resulting decision benefits the organization or team as a whole.

Two cautions in doing this: first, don't say "I'm putting the best interest of the team over my own." When you say this, it sounds as if you're doing the team a favor and trying to "sell" them on a decision. Second, don't try to back into why a decision which benefits you as a leader is also good for the organization or team. The team can see through it in a heartbeat and you'll continue to hurt your credibility.

 Graduating with honors:
Leaders who take action with integrity are able to create loyal, hard-working, effective teams that deliver results and make customers and stakeholders happy. Take away the leader's integrity and the team may perform, but certainly not to the same level as a team whose action-oriented leader maintains a high level of integrity. Earn the team's trust by taking the *question* out of *questionable* integrity.

I n September, Jane was elected PTA president for her daughter's elementary school. Her first few meetings with her PTA board went very well. There were a lot of great ideas generated for how to raise funds for the school and the board members all seemed very excited about the upcoming activities.

Jane and the board decided to hold an auction in April to raise money for the school, selling auction items made by the students or donated by local businesses. Jane had hoped to raise $30,000 from the auction and personally took on the task of managing the auction. In her eagerness, Jane started assigning tasks to board members. Although many of the members were unsure of Jane's overall plan, they still maintained some trust that she knew what she was doing.

Subsequent meetings became a replay of the last meeting: Jane assigned tasks to board members without a clear connection to an overall plan. The board members reluctantly took on the various tasks. Finally, at the March meeting one of the board members, Ellen, asked Jane to define the remaining tasks to be done in order for the auction to be a success in April. As Jane and the board began defining the remaining work, they discovered to their dismay that the earliest they could hold the auction would be July. In looking at the work that had already been completed by the board members, many of the tasks appeared to have little relation to the auction. The board ultimately decided not to have the auction. Jane's exuberance and desire for *activity* without *focus* created *randomness* among the team.

Learning the Lesson:

Leading a team means setting a meaningful objective, understanding how to achieve the objective, inspiring the team to complete the objective, and leading them down the field to victory. With each of these steps, the leader is expected to maintain a razor-sharp focus on what needs to be done. Think about a pro football (American football to my non-U.S. friends!) quarterback. His job is clear; to move the ball down the field until the ball (attached to a player) crosses over the goal line. The successful quarterback maintains focus and keeps the ball moving through a variety of passing and running plays. If he loses that focus, there is greater likelihood for fumbles or turnovers which keep the quarterback from achieving his objective. It's no different when leading a team. Define the objective, plan out the work to achieve the objective, inspire the team, and execute.

What are some of the barriers to keeping strong focus and driving the team to results? Try these on for size:

- **The objective isn't clear** – Maybe the objective is too nebulous, i.e., "to achieve complete customer satisfaction," improbable, "to solve world hunger by next month," or random, "to solve all of our management problems." A poorly articulated objective sets a weak foundation for the team which then results in random performance.

- **The plan isn't clear** – Even with well-articulated objectives, if the plan to achieve the objective doesn't make sense, then the team will flail around wondering what they are supposed to do to meet the objective. In absence of a good plan, the team will either start making up the plan on the fly or will ultimately stagnate while waiting for the leader to provide clear direction.

- **The leader keeps getting distracted** – So there's a great objective defined, and a good plan is laid out. Then the leader gets an acute case of "shiny object syndrome." After every meeting, phone call, or hallway discussion, the leader diverts from the plan and starts swimming towards a new shiny object. The team now is unsure of direction because there frankly isn't any. It is "direction du jour" played out in real life for all to see.

- **The team doesn't believe in the objective** – Even if the objective and plan are clearly articulated and the leader makes his best effort to keep the team focused, they can still lose focus if they don't believe the objective is the right thing to do. Now, rather than having a well-oiled, results-oriented team, the team operates in fits and starts with periodic statements of, "Why are we doing this again?"

- **The team doesn't have the tools it needs to get the job done** – Imagine sending an army into battle equipped with pea shooters and sling shots. All the makings of the quickest battle in history. Similarly, tasking a team with a stretch goal without equipping them with the tools they need to get things done is recipe for random, disjointed execution.

Before we get too deep, I want to put forth a caution on focus. Focus taken to an extreme can morph into stubbornness. Recently I was watching a TV show where a young doctor was doggedly trying to revive a patient whose heart had stopped beating. The doctor kept giving CPR to the patient for over 30 minutes in hopes of reviving the patient. Everyone else knew that the patient had died, but the young doctor persisted. Finally, a more senior doctor had to tell the young doctor to stop because nothing more could be done. Leaders and teams can also be focused to the point of stubbornness where *continuing on the current path is no longer the right thing to do.* The leader needs to ensure that focus is balanced with common sense and periodically checks himself to verify that the team is moving in the right direction toward an achievable objective.

Adding it up:
Securing and maintaining focus and avoiding the randomness beast isn't all that difficult; it just means creating some discipline:

- **Get clear with the objective** – Define a concise, believable objective which articulates *what* needs to be done, *when* it needs to be done by, and *what measure* you will use to determine if the objective is met. A statement such as "We want to raise $30,000 through a PTA auction by April 15" defines the *what* (PTA Auction), *when* (April 15), and *what measure* ($30,000).

- **Define a simple plan which everyone understands** – Design a simple plan or task list which clearly articulates for each task *what* needs to be done, *who* needs to do it, and *when* it needs to be done by. A good rule of thumb is to keep task length to one week or less, and ensure that one team member can be assigned to the task. If the task is longer than one week or if multiple people are needed to complete the task, then break the task into smaller amounts until both rules of thumb are met.

- **Decide upon the scope of your objective –** Think about a fútbol field (that is soccer for my U.S. friends!). The field has boundary lines which define play as being "in-bounds" or "out-of-bounds." When defining your objective, you need to consciously determine what will be "in-bounds" (things you will focus on as part of your work) and "out-of-bounds" (things you will not focus on). Getting clarity on the scope will help you with shiny object syndrome. Speaking of which….

- **Beware of "shiny objects" –** Look, issues will crop up while executing your plan. Don't stick your head in the sand and ignore the issues, but don't get distracted with issues that don't need to be addressed by you or the team. Sure, you can argue that the issue is important and needs to be addressed, but if it falls outside of the scope of what you are doing then set it aside.

 Graduating with honors:
Creating and maintaining focus while moving your team toward a stated objective is crucial to getting things done on time.

When you have a clearly stated objective and scope, an easy-to-understand plan, and protect the team from shiny objects, you significantly increase your likelihood of success. Ignore these tips and you'll brand yourself as random which means quite frankly, no one will want to follow you. Move with focus and get work done.

Why Don't They Follow Me?

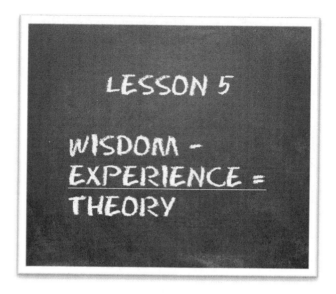

LESSON 5

WISDOM -
EXPERIENCE =
THEORY

Greg was a new employee at a large multinational corporation. He had just graduated at the top of his class from a prestigious university and was very well read on a wide variety of leadership topics. His success in college allowed Greg to enter his new job confidently and gave him the self-assurance he felt he needed to take on big assignments at his new job.

At a weekly staff meeting, Greg's manager, Hal, asked for someone to take on a short-term project to manage a team of vendors to successfully put on a large event for some of the company's most important customers. Greg eagerly jumped at the opportunity and convinced his manager to give him the assignment. Using all of his know-how he learned in school, Greg set out to plan the project, assign resources, and define due-dates. All appeared to be going well, then reality hit....

The first blow came when the chosen vendor didn't staff the project with experienced personnel. The second came when the facility where the event was to be housed unexpectedly shut down due to structural problems. Rather than asking for help, Greg took on an "I can do this on my own" attitude and relied upon his knowledge to solve problems he had no experience with. Time ticked by and Greg still tried to muscle through the problems on his own. Ultimately, Hal recognized that Greg wasn't going to be successful and assigned the project to one of Greg's more experienced peers. Greg was crushed. The next day Greg met with Hal and got some very wise advice. "Greg, you're very smart and have a lot of great skills," Hal said, "but the best leaders are able to leverage their smarts with either their own experience or the experience of colleagues to get things done effectively. You relied on your own knowledge to accomplish this task, and were reluctant to seek out the experience of others to help you. That decision ultimately cost you the assignment."

 Learning the Lesson:
So I'm going to set expectations on this up front: having a theoretical under-

standing of a topic is a very good thing. Whether it's theories on leadership, marketing, or manufacturing, having a good perspective on different theories dramatically broadens a leader's horizons and arms her with additional tools to do her job more successfully. However, I do believe that for a leader to truly be effective at leading others and have the wisdom to lead, that theory needs to be tightly coupled with experience. I can sit and watch the greatest golfers in the world sink 30-foot putts time after time but I need to get out there and do it myself, using what I've learned from the greats, to improve my putting game.

So how can inexperienced leaders run into problems? Look at these and see what you think:

- **Not having an experienced mentor to provide counsel** – A leader without an experienced, trusted colleague to turn to for advice is like someone flying an airplane and knowing what only half of those tiny buttons and knobs in the cockpit do. Not gleaning the benefit of a colleague's experience on tough issues unnecessarily hampers the inexperienced leader's ability to lead.

- **Not *wanting* an experienced mentor to provide counsel** – Ooh, very different problem. This isn't about a pilot not *knowing* what half of those tiny buttons and knobs in the cockpit do; it's about the pilot not *caring* what they do. These young hot-shots (yes, I was one) feel they've got it all together and that they're going to teach the rest of the world how to do things right. It took a couple of huge failures for me to recognize that having a mentor wasn't a sign of weakness; it was a sign of wisdom.

- **Not knowing what to do when things go wrong** – Experience coupled with theory becomes crucial, not necessarily when things are going *right*, but when things start going *wrong*. Many young leaders know the rudiments of leadership cold: define the objective, plan out the work, assemble the team, assign tasks, and monitor the schedule. Because they know the rudiments (or theory), they assume they could navigate any team to do anything. Then something goes wrong; maybe an unforeseen issue, a team member not performing to expectation, or a manager reassigning some of the team members to another project. This is where application of theory goes awry because real-life problems crept into the theoretical world. Painful times.

- **Not learning from past mistakes** – Let's do a little test. Go into your kitchen. Turn on the stove. Wait two minutes. Now, put your hand on the stove. Hot? Now, do it all over again. Still hot? Hopefully you didn't take me seriously here, but you get the point. I'm amazed at the leaders I've seen who make the same mistake multiple times hoping for a different result. Mistakes are part of the learning experience, but shouldn't need to be learned over and over again.

- **Being afraid to venture out of a comfort zone for fear of failure** – Remember learning how to ride a bike? Certainly you fell a few times and maybe skinned a knee or elbow. Eventually you learned to ride and now it's like second nature. Inexperienced leaders need to get out and try things. They need the opportunity to skin a knee or elbow. They also need to start small. When an inexperienced leader takes on a high-stakes project or leading a large complex team, the stakes of failure become much greater. This is akin to learning how to ride a bike on a busy street. The stakes of failure are much greater than a skinned knee; the inexperienced rider can be hit by a car and be injured far greater than if he or she learned to ride in a cul-de-sac or empty parking lot.

Adding it up:

Leveraging and gaining leadership experience is crucial for any leader regardless of experience level. The more experienced (and secure) I become, the more I look to others for advice and counsel. Try these few tips out to build your experiencing arsenal:

- **Get a mentor** – Regardless of whether you are a brand new leader or you have been leading for years, find at least one colleague you can bounce ideas off of and benefit from his experience. I have several colleagues I meet with regularly to share ideas, get feedback, and learn from their counsel.

- **Keep a lessons-learned log** – As you continue to gain more experience as a leader, keep a log of what is working for you as a leader and what isn't. For the items that are working for you, keep improving upon them. For those that aren't working for you, use your mentor to help you understand where the problem areas lie.

- **Get out of your comfort zone** – Take on a task with which you aren't completely comfortable. Maybe it's leading a larger team than you've led in the past, or a project which has a couple of unique challenges. One technique I have used successfully is to "leverage a skill to learn a skill." For example, I took on a new job which required strong project management skills (my area of expertise) in a functional area which I wasn't familiar. I was able to bring good project management discipline to the table and at the same time learned a ton about a new functional area. I put a lot of new tools into my wisdom toolbox while at the same time provided some immediate value to my new organization.

Graduating with honors:

Having the wisdom of Solomon requires establishing a strong knowledge base coupled with the practical experience of learning by doing. Having a trusted mentor, learning from past mistakes through a lessons-learned log, and getting out of your comfort zone are great means of applying theoretical knowledge to real-life situations. Just remember to keep building wisdom through experience and theory and to share your wisdom with others by being a mentor to colleagues and less-experienced leaders.

Why Don't They Follow Me?

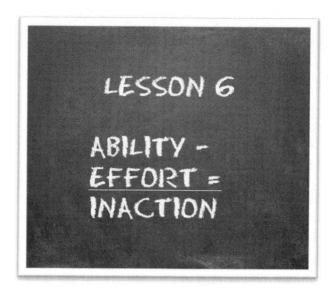

LESSON 6

ABILITY -
EFFORT =
INACTION

J anet had just walked out of an interview with Bill, a prospective employee. She was very impressed with Bill's command of the subject matter and believed his experience would be a welcome addition to the group. Janet offered Bill the job and he readily accepted.

After Bill was on the job a few weeks, Janet noticed a disturbing trend. While Bill was great at providing advice and counsel to others, he didn't seem to put much effort into his work and was always looking for the easy way out on his assignments. Janet noticed that Bill would bring assignments to her which appeared half-completed hoping she would accept them as complete. Although she was thankful to have Bill's expertise in the group, she was concerned about the lack of effort he put into his work.

After several months, Janet needed a team leader to lead a small project assigned by her manager. After much thought, Janet chose Brenda, one of Bill's peers, as the team leader and put Bill on the project as a subject matter expert reporting to Brenda. Bill was disappointed and asked Janet to explain why he wasn't chosen for the job. Janet told Bill point blank, "Bill, you've got great ability and I love your command of subject matter, but I'm concerned that you aren't going to put in the effort to get the job done right. My boss is very concerned that the project is a success so I need to have someone leading the project who will get it done, which is why I chose Brenda. Bill, to be a great leader you need to balance your abilities with effort."

 Learning the Lesson:
This one is easy; there is truly no such thing as a free lunch; whatever you do is going to take hard work, perseverance, and willingness to achieve your goal. There are few things more frustrating to me as a leader and coach than seeing a leader-in-the-making with outstanding abilities, a strong knowledge base, and a great network of mentors and coaches, who squanders the opportunity because she is unwilling to put forth the necessary effort to grow as a leader.

When looking at this a bit deeper, though, there are a few reasons those who have the *ability* to do something may not put forth the *effort* to get it done, as follows:

- **The leader doesn't want to work hard** – Obviously. The leader looks for others to do the work for him or only does the absolute minimum amount of work to get by. Lazy lazy lazy.

- **The leader lacks confidence** – Maybe a leader truly wants to exercise her ability and work hard, but is fearful of failure or is concerned about looking foolish to colleagues, friends, or the boss. Having a healthy fear during execution is normal and expected; having a fear which paralyzes the leader into inaction is cause for concern.

- **The leader wants to put forth the effort, but doesn't know what to do** – Maybe the effort required to complete a task is a bit out of a leader's skill set and the leader is unsure how to proceed. The desire is there and the leader is willing to put the hard work in to make it happen, but doesn't know where to go to figure out how to get the task done.

 Adding it up:
Having the desire to put in the effort needed to get tasks done breathes life

into your ability and can help make you an action-oriented leader. Follow some simple tips to help you up the effort curve:

- **Realign your expectations** – Time to be honest with yourself. If you like taking the easy way out and look to just meet the minimum to get something done, then it's time to adjust your effort meter. I'm not advocating that you burn yourself out with work to demonstrate your effort; but understand what is needed to get a job done well and on time and gauge your effort to meet the delivery expectation.

- **Use a mentor or coach** – A mentor or coach can help validate ideas and help give you the confidence you need to put forth the effort to get things done. Your mentor or coach is there to help you solve your problems, not solve them for you; don't dump problems on his or her doorstep to solve. Ask your mentor or coach plenty of questions even if you think the question is dumb; the only dumb question is truly the one that doesn't get asked.

- **Do some research** – In this wonderful internet age we live in, vast amounts of information are only an e-click away. For most any problem you encounter you can probably find information on the problem and resolution via the internet. Take a bit of time to research your problem and get a read on how others might have addressed the problem.

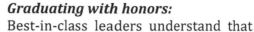 ***Graduating with honors:***
Best-in-class leaders understand that effort needs to complement ability to truly get things done. If you have an issue with motivating yourself to put forth effort then it's high time you realign your expectations and get on the effort bandwagon. Use a mentor or coach to bounce ideas off of and do some research to learn how others addressed the issue you're dealing with. Coupling your ability with effort will take you out of the inactive column and make you the action-oriented leader you want to be.

Why Don't They Follow Me?

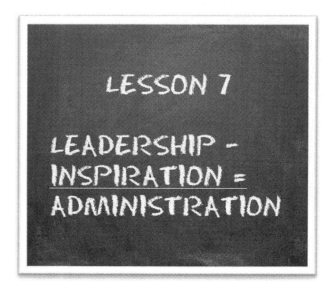

LESSON 7

LEADERSHIP -
INSPIRATION =
ADMINISTRATION

S am is a very experienced manager who just accepted a new position running a customer support call center for a medical supplies manufacturer. Sam has managed organizations ranging in size from several people to several hundred people. His style of leadership has always been one of command and control. He tended to dole out tasks to his team and micromanage the execution of the tasks until the work was complete. Monica, the manager who Sam replaced, was recently promoted to vice president and is now Sam's boss. Monica's style of leadership was more about inspiring the team through direction setting, joint planning with the team, empowering the team to deliver, and coaching through the execution.

Sam had been on the job about four weeks when the defections started. Those team members who were used to Monica's inspirational style of leadership were now subject to Sam's command and control style. While some of the team just sucked it up and stayed in the organization, the drop in productivity was dramatic. Several of the team members approached Monica about Sam's leadership style. Monica decided to take action.

Monica scheduled a meeting with Sam to discuss the drop in productivity and some of the reasons for the drop. Sam clearly held to a view that the productivity drop was due to the change in leadership and that things would get better as the team got more used to him. Though Monica was skeptical, she agreed to let Sam try to work things out. Two months went by; productivity was still down and the attrition rate was higher than ever. Monica approached Sam about the continued drop in productivity. Sam in so many words told Monica that he knew how to manage teams and let him do his thing. Monica had seen enough and decided to replace Sam. His inability to inspire the team and his command and control method of leadership ultimately resulted in his removal.

Learning the Lesson:
In this leadership lesson I want to discuss what I view as the most important characteristic of a leader; the ability to

inspire a team to deliver. Leaders who inspire a team to deliver do the following:

- Paint a clear, compelling picture of the objective which needs to be met and when it needs to be done by.
- Articulate a plan for how the team is to get from point to destination.
- Encourage team members to own portions of the plan and be responsible for successful completion.
- Remove barriers which hold the team up.
- Coach team members to help them be more effective.
- Take an avid interest in learning and encourage the team to broaden their horizons.
- Praise calculated risk taking.
- Celebrate wins with the team.

As a leader, I knew that I had achieved a level of inspiration when the team didn't need me around to execute. The team truly felt empowered to drive the work, make decisions, and deliver results. Rather than giving direction, I was used to break down barriers, provide counsel, enforce accountability, and help the team members wrestle through tough issues. Leading an inspired team is incredibly easy because the team is doing the work and the leader is assisting the team. Magical.

When inspiration is removed from the leadership equation, the team takes on a very different composition. Rather than being truly empowered to deliver results, the team is reduced to running errands for the administrator and providing information so the administrator can do his or her job. The team may or may not know what the information is going to be used for or why it is needed; all they know is that the administrator needs it by a certain date. Rather than feeling ownership over their work, there is more of an "I do it because I have to" mentality. Given the choice, most people who work under an administrator would choose to not work for the administrator.

So what causes some leaders to have difficulty achieving an inspiration level of leadership? Here are a few reasons:

- **Trust** – A leader has to trust that a team will deliver results. If the leader has issues with trust, or the team members haven't proven themselves trustworthy, the leader will have difficulty empowering the team members.

- **Confidence** – A leader who isn't confident in her own ability to deliver results will want to control more of the work to ensure it is meeting her expectations. A leader with a confidence issue may also be leery of a team member showing her up and creating a power struggle between the leader and the team member. The team can sense the lack of confidence in the leader and will be reluctant to follow him.

- **Inexperience** – Frankly, it is difficult (not impossible) for an inexperienced leader to create an empowerment environment because the leader simply doesn't have enough experience to coach, mentor, and guide the team.

- **Leadership Stereotypes** – Many leaders today still operate under a command and control model because they think that's just what leaders do. While many leaders pay lip service to inspiring a team, those same leaders will slip more into a command and control mode of leadership especially when things start going wrong.

I want to be careful to cast inspiration in its proper light. Inspiring a team still means setting and enforcing direction and giving the team the tools it needs to succeed. At the end of the day, the leader is still accountable for achieving results. Thus, a leader can't just let a team do whatever they please and expect to be successful. The leader needs to provide the direction, paint the base-paths, guide the execution, and help the team when trouble erupts.

 Adding it up:
Moving from an administrative leader to an inspirational leader requires putting several things in place, as follows:

- **Put competent people in key positions** – If your team is too junior, has the wrong skill set, or is unwilling to be empowered, then no amount of inspirational leading is going to deliver results. Decide where you have competency gaps in your team and put the right people in those positions.

- **Assess your own strengths and weaknesses** – As a leader, you may need to work on trust, self-confidence, courage and conviction, or other key leadership attributes. Self-assess your strengths and weaknesses and decide which weaknesses to hit first.

- **Practice inspirational leadership on smaller projects or tasks** – Just as with any other skill set, you need to learn some new habits to shift from an administrative leader to an inspirational leader. Take on a small project and practice setting direction, developing a plan, establishing ownership over pieces of the plan, and playing the role of coach during execution. As you get more comfortable with the new skills, increase the scope to other projects, then to your entire team.

- **Get some coaching** – You may see yourself in one light, yet others may see you in a very different light. Use a coach or mentor to help you identify situations where you are leading as an administrator rather than a leader who inspires. In-the-moment feedback can be highly beneficial for you and help you improve as a leader.

Graduating with honors:
As leaders, we are given the responsibility to perform a job and are (hopefully) given commensurate authority to perform that job. How we use that authority with our team can be radically different depending on our leadership style. When we as leaders inspire our teams to perform by setting direction, painting the base-paths, empowering them to deliver, and coaching the execution, we deliver far better results than those leaders who administer through command and control. Inspire people to perform, then get out of the way and watch the magic happen.

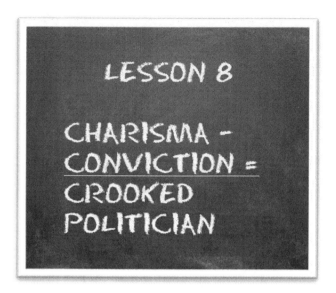

LESSON 8

CHARISMA -
CONVICTION =
CROOKED
POLITICIAN

Alfred is that typical guy everyone likes. He's friendly, funny, articulate, and witty. He can always be counted on to break up a room when things are tense and is the life of the party at social events. He's just your all-around fun guy to be around.

Alfred's boss, Karen, asked him to take a new job as a team leader of a small organization. Everyone in the organization liked Alfred so Karen thought there was little risk to Alfred taking on the assignment. Alfred accepted the job.

As Alfred settled into the position, things seemed to go great with the team. They agreed upon objectives, defined the work, and set out to meet the objectives. Alfred also was very vocal about the team working whatever shifts they wanted to work, so long as the work got done. The team loved Alfred's flexibility and responded very favorably.

As time went on, Alfred began scheduling mandatory meetings for all team members at 7 a.m. each morning. These meetings were "no-excuses" meetings, meaning that everyone had to be there. This created a problem with a number of the team members who didn't come in until after noon because of commitments outside of work. Alfred didn't care; he still expected those people at the 7 a.m. meetings even if it meant going back home and coming in later in the afternoon for their regular shift. Similar situations came up where Alfred expected team members to be at work during certain times of the day. What started off as a very promising relationship between Alfred and the team turned into one of contentiousness and confusion. While Alfred had tremendous charisma and a personal connection to his team, he turned into a poor leader because his team couldn't trust his convictions.

Learning the Lesson:
When it comes to conviction, a leader must articulate two very important facets about his conviction. First, he needs to

articulate his job-related *principles.* For example, the leader may be very passionate about cultivating future leaders, keeping work/life balance, or maintaining open and honest communication among the team. The second, and more important, facet of conviction is the leader needs to demonstrate that he is *loyal* to the principles he maintains. You may think of this as whether or not the leader "walks the talk" when it comes to his principles. For example, if a leader espouses a principle of maintaining a healthy work/life balance yet expects his or her team to put in 70+ hour weeks on a regular basis, then the principle of work/life balance is only window dressing. The leader isn't loyal to his principle. When a leader definitively declares his principles and demonstrates a loyalty toward keeping them, he exemplifies a believable conviction which team members can rely on through thick and thin.

While a leader may hold strong convictions, the next step is for the leader and the team to understand where the convictions of the leader differ from those of individual team members. For example, I was considering working for an organization in which the team leader maintained a very strong conviction that employees needed to do whatever it took to meet deadlines, regardless of the sacrifice to family. He demonstrated this conviction by scheduling 7 p.m. meetings as well as Saturday morning meetings. His convictions were very clear, but they did not match my own convictions. I ended up not working for that organization, but was thankful that the convictions were out there for me to see and ultimately decide whether or not to make a job change.

Where do leaders have difficulty in the conviction department? Give these a look:

- **Convictions are not clearly stated or understood** – A leader may have some convictions but be afraid or reluctant to divulge them to his team. Rather than expose something which might be controversial or embarrassing, the leader chooses to straddle the fence and not take a position.

- **Convictions change too frequently** – A leader whose convictions change direction whenever political winds blow or when a leader receives a new boss really has nothing worth anchoring onto. Those chameleon-like leaders tend to frustrate the team because they can never reliably align their own convictions to those of the leader's. One day, they may love their job because of aligned convictions; the next day they may hate it because a conviction-shift occurred.

- **The leader doesn't "walk the talk"** – As I explained earlier, a leader may say all of the right things, such as placing a high value on work/life balance, but his actions contradict the principle. Not only does this put the leader's convictions in question, it also damages his or her integrity.

Adding it up:

Your convictions as a leader aren't something you want your team to question. A leader's convictions speak to the foundation upon which the leader makes decisions and drives the priorities of both him and the team. Take time to put some things in place to develop rock-solid convictions:

- **Do some serious principles soul searching** – Take some time to truly understand what is important to you and where your passion lies. Don't make this a cerebral, what-do-people-want-me-to-say activity. Be honest with yourself on what principles are important to you. You also may consider enlisting the help of a spouse, significant other, friend, or colleague to help you understand your principles.

- **Declare your convictions** – Once you clearly understand and are comfortable with your convictions, make sure your team very clearly understands what they are. Your convictions may align with some team members and not with others; but it's better to make an overt declaration which you and your team members can understand than keep everyone guessing which page you are really on.

- **Once you declare, stick to them –** Convictions shouldn't go in and out of style like the width of neckties; they are meant to be anchors about you on which others can rely. Having said this, we all are growing older and our priorities are changing. If you see a fundamental shift in your convictions, then you should by all means revise your convictions and re-declare them to your team.

- **Walk the talk –** By now you hopefully get the point on this; don't let team members question your convictions because your actions don't match what you say.

Graduating with honors:
A leader's convictions are a cornerstone of who he is as a person, what he sees as important, how he makes decisions, and what priorities he works to. Leaders who are very charismatic but have unstable or nonexistent belief systems are prone to say whatever the crowd wants to hear out of fear of losing popularity or a desire to be voted back into office. Convictions aren't about being popular, funny or mainstream. They are about what is important to you as a leader and person. Understand your convictions, state them, commit to them, and live them. Your team may not agree with your convictions, but they will appreciate knowing where you stand and in the long run will have greater trust and respect for you as a leader.

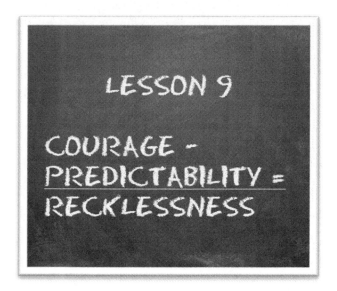

LESSON 9

COURAGE -
PREDICTABILITY =
RECKLESSNESS

Joe's nickname was "Captain Courageous." When he was a child, Joe was always the one who would jump off a cliff into a pool of water or race dirt bikes. He seemed to have no fear and would try anything.

As Joe grew into an adult, his courage and risk-taking stayed with him and showed itself in his leadership skills. He had no fear of high-risk projects or deadlines his peers wouldn't touch with a ten-foot pole. While his courage was admired by his manager Sandy, she was concerned about his motivations for taking on these tough challenges. It appeared that Joe achieved a "high" by taking on tough projects and he seemed to sign up for risky ventures primarily for the thrill of it. While Joe was very *courageous*, his *predictability* as a leader was questionable due to his lack of stability in his beliefs. Joe's *courage* was overshadowed by a perception of *recklessness.* Joe's progression as a leader was ultimately stunted because he was viewed as reckless.

Learning the Lesson:
The movie *Gladiator* is one of my favorite flicks. One of the most memorable scenes is when Maximus, played by Russell Crowe, announces before marching into battle *"At my signal, unleash hell."* Maximus simply oozed courage as he uttered the line. Just as importantly, he was singular, focused, and *predictable* in his mission; to annihilate the barbarians. There was no need to second-guess his motivations, and his army responded by following Maximus into victory.

Team members love to see a leader who is willing to defend and protect his or her team. There is a security the team feels when they know their leader won't abandon them or hang them out to dry. For that feeling of security to be realized, the team needs to understand the leader's intentions and know how *predictable* the leader will be when his or her courage is put to the test. Those leaders who consistently stick to their beliefs garner a tremendous degree of trust from the team; those whose responses vary with the roll of the dice keep the team off balance and never achieve a high degree of trust with the team.

There are some significant predictability barriers that label courageous leaders as reckless, as follows:

- **The leader's beliefs are unknown –** We talked about convictions in the previous lesson. Just as a boat that isn't anchored will drift in the sea, a leader with unknown beliefs will drift in his or her actions.

- **The leader has difficulty controlling emotions –** Leaders who take action out of highly charged emotions such as anger, fear, or glee can create distrust with the team. When emotions drive a leader's actions, the leader is demonstrating that his actions can vary based on mood and impact the team in different ways, solely dependent on that mood.

- **The leader becomes emotionally tied to a solution –** Having passion about a particular solution is great, but when a leader becomes passionate to a point where her predictability is questioned, then reckless decisions are apt to follow. Belief-based predictability morphs into passion-based unpredictability.

 Adding it up:
Predictability that is based on sound beliefs is a mandatory requirement for

the courageous leader. As a courageous leader, put the following in place to avoid the reckless label:

- **State your beliefs** – When the team knows where you stand on your beliefs, some of the guesswork is taken out of how you make decisions, which strengthens your predict-tability. Don't hide them; let them be known.

- **Take stock of yourself when emotions are out of check** – Take a reality check on how you behave when your emotions are out of check. Do you make snap decisions when you're angry? Are you more likely to agree to something when you're feeling happy versus sad? If you're having difficulty with self-assessing, use a spouse, significant other, or colleague to help you.

- **Take a time-out** – If you feel you're not in a good frame of mind to drive belief-based decisions or direction, give yourself a few minutes to bring your emotions back in line. A brisk walk or a quiet cup of coffee can help realign your mind and bring more predictability to your direction.

- **Sleep on it** – This is particularly difficult for highly action-oriented leaders (guilty as charged!). When faced with a challenging decision or a major direction change, give yourself a good night's sleep to muddle through it and bounce it against your beliefs.

- **Ask for opinions** – I can't stress this enough. Garnering the wisdom of others helps shape your thinking and enhances your predictability as a leader. Taking a predictable action of asking for other opinions in your decision making or direction setting process reinforces your predictability as a leader.

Graduating with honors:
Team members will follow a courageous leader before they would follow a cowardly lion. The willingness to follow becomes tarnished, though, when the leader doesn't demonstrate predictability in his thought process. Demonstrate predictability by communicating your beliefs and avoiding emotion-driven decisions and direction-setting and you'll keep recklessness off of your list of things to work on.

Why Don't They Follow Me?

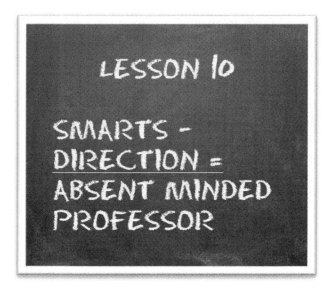

LESSON 10

SMARTS –
DIRECTION =
ABSENT MINDED
PROFESSOR

I once worked for a manager who was one of the smartest people I had ever met. He had a Ph.D. from a very prestigious university and could think in dimensions I could only hope to understand before I died. I was in awe of his intellectual horsepower and pure knowledge.

What I wasn't in awe of was his lack of desire to establish and communicate a cohesive direction for the team. In his own mind he truly believed that both he and everyone else understood the direction he wanted to take the organization. The truth was that we as a team had absolutely no clue where he wanted to take the organization. Worse still, he would get very irritated when we tried to pin him down on direction. So, while I was highly impressed by his intellectual horsepower, I had great difficulty with the lack of a clear understanding of his desired direction.

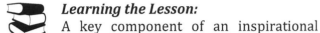 ***Learning the Lesson:***
A key component of an inspirational leader is one who drives a clear and believable direction for the team to follow. Whether it affects thousands of people in a multinational corporation or only a handful of people in a volunteer organization, establishing a direction which motivates and inspires a team to deliver results is a crucial first step to being an inspirational leader.

So what does setting direction really mean? To me, setting direction means answering four basic questions:

1. Where do you want to go?
2. When do you want to get there?
3. How will you get there?
4. How will you know you are there?

Think about these four questions in planning your next vacation. You need to know where you want go (Disneyland), when you want to get there (July 4th) how you're going to get there (drive), and how you will know you are there (get your picture taken with Mickey). If all goes as planned, you've successfully arrived at Disneyland to see the fireworks; everyone is well rested and fed and the kids are still talking to each other.

Where do leaders have difficulty in direction setting? Here are a few barriers:

- **The leader has poor direction setting skills** – Let's face it; some leaders just don't have good direction setting skills. Maybe they weren't in environments where direction setting was stressed, or they didn't have a good mentor or coach to help build direction setting skills. Or, maybe they are used to developing direction without the input and buy-in of the team.

- **Direction setting isn't viewed as "real work"** – I've heard some leaders downplay the importance of direction setting because tactical work wasn't getting done. When a leader is under deadlines to deliver a result, things like direction setting tend to be pushed to the bottom of the to-do list.

- **A direction is set, but it changes too frequently** – A leader may set a direction which has all of the right components, but if he changes direction to the point that the team experiences "direction du jour syndrome," then the team is really no better off than having no direction at all.

- **A direction is set, but not followed** – A leader can do all the right things to set direction, but if they are not followed, then all the work was a massive waste of time. Many times a leader will set direction because it is required by his organization or management, not because he believes it is important.

- **The leader delegates direction setting** – Nope, no can do. I've heard leaders say they want to empower their teams by allowing a lieutenant to drive direction setting. I believe when a leader delegates direction setting, he is sending a message that direction setting isn't important enough to do it himself.

Adding it up:
Setting a clear, concise, and believable direction is an important skill for a leader and is crucial to getting a team moving in the right direction. Use some of these tips to help you be a great direction setter:

- **Be participative in developing your direction** – Setting the direction for a team is something the entire team should understand, remember, and execute to. Include your organization in the direction settings to ensure you get the buy-in you need. Just remember that it is your responsibility as a leader to own setting direction.

- **Be cautious about jump-starting the process with your own direction viewpoint** – Depending on the team, this either works well or not so well. If your team is bold, engaged, and not afraid to question, then you can probably come in with something and let the team shoot holes at it. If your team isn't as bold or might be afraid to question you, then you're better off starting with a blank slate and doing the discovery process together.

- **Review your direction regularly** – Priorities do change within an organization; a key problem arises when the team's direction doesn't change with the new priorities. I've certainly been guilty of setting a direction at the beginning of the fiscal year then never looking at it again. Keep it available, review it monthly, and ensure it reflects the current plan.

- **Measure progress against the direction you set** – On a monthly or quarterly basis, provide a status of results achieved that support your team direction. Presumably you developed the direction to drive your team toward specific results, so why not show the team and other stakeholders how you're doing based on what you said you would do?

Graduating with honors:
Having great intelligence and know-ledge as a leader is important to establishing credibility and showing a team that you have the intellectual horsepower to lead the team. But a leader needs to couple that

intelligence with the discipline to establish and drive the team's direction to deliver results. Take direction out of the equation and you end up with a really bright person with runaway intellect and a team without purpose.

LESSON 11

COMMUNICATION -
CANDOR =
STORYTELLER

A number of years back I worked for a very senior manager at my company. He was not only a charismatic leader but was also an excellent communicator. He was very articulate, concise, and believable. Every presentation he delivered was simply captivating. He was and is very impressive.

One thing that I noticed about this manager was that his communication was not only polished, it was also very candid. If he had bad news to deliver, he delivered it. If he screwed something up, he would say "I screwed up." His candor significantly boosted his credibility and created an environment where team members wanted to follow him as a leader. His straight-shooter style of communication was highly respected across the entire organization.

 Learning the Lesson:
Many leaders, particularly in these times of political correctness, pad their communication with soft statements, sugar-coated platitudes, or watered-down messages. Many times this is out of concern for insulting someone, being the bearer of bad news, or political backlash. The best communicators I have seen, though, express themselves in a very forthright, respectful, and sincere manner. Rather than search for the perfect phrase, they tell it like it is, even if it makes them look bad as a result. Their *candor* didn't always win them points in a popularity contest, but it was always more appreciated than a message which appeared less than sincere.

What causes a leader to not be completely candid in his or her communication? Here are a few points:

- **Fear of insulting or offending someone** – Maybe the leader is concerned about offending a recipient of the communication. Then again, the person who is the subject of the communication could be insulted if the messaging is wrong.

- **Concern over a personal backlash** – A leader may be overly sensitive or fearful of how she will be perceived as a result of a difficult communication. Phrases like, "I had a lapse in judgment," or, "because of my indiscretion," contain as much sincerity as a can of candied yams.

- **There's more to the story** – Certainly there are times when confidentiality needs to be respected, particularly regarding communications about people. When facts are consciously omitted to the point that a communication is a watered-down worthless message, speculation about "the rest of the story" abounds through grapevine fodder.

 Adding it up:
Leaders who sprinkle communications with fairy dust hoping to avoid difficult issues or avert personal backlash raise questions about their authenticity and integrity. Demonstrate sincere, respectful candor in your communication by putting some of these tips to work for you:

- **Say it straight** – If you've got something to say, just say it. Do your best to be respectful and professional, and definitely don't use profanity or offensive statements. This is particularly important if you've screwed something up. Saying, "The project overrun was due to my underestimating the cost of the project," sounds more sincere than, "I regret that a lapse in judgment may have contributed to a temporary reduction in profitability." Have the courage to tell it like it is.

- **Start from the candid statement** – When composing a communication with sensitive content, start with the candid, direct, un-sanitized message, then write a cleaned-up version. After you've cleaned up your messaging, compare it to your original message. Do you still believably get your point across or is it just a bunch of psycho-babble?

- **Ask a coach or colleague to review your communication prior to delivery** – Do you have a piece of communication which you're concerned about how it will be perceived? Send it to a coach or colleague beforehand and get her blunt reaction. Does it sound authentic or like a load of manure? Is it disrespectful? Is it so watered down that it will cause huge grapes to sprout on the grapevine? Getting a straightforward reaction will help you increase the effectiveness of your communication.

Graduating with honors:
A leader who communicates with candor not only demonstrates high integrity, but also exemplifies courage. Delivering results isn't always about communicating shiny, happy messages. Straight talk is necessary to ensure there are no misunderstandings and that recipients don't fill

in the blanks on their own with grapevine chatter. Subtract candor from your communication equation, and you'll get your picture hung in the Aesop's Fables Hall of Fame.

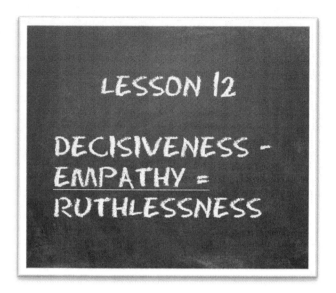

LESSON 12

DECISIVENESS -
EMPATHY =
RUTHLESSNESS

colleague of mine was asked to be an interim CEO of a medium-sized company while the board of directors searched for a permanent CEO. This company had its share of growing pains and was now facing some difficult decisions in order to cut expenses. My colleague, along with the board of directors, decided that about 200 people needed to be laid off for the company to survive. This involved massively difficult choices that would affect the lives of many people. My colleague decided to personally meet with every employee to be laid off and explain why the layoff was needed. In doing so, he also wanted the employees to know how he hated making such a decision but that it was necessary for the company to stay afloat.

Think about this for a minute. Imagine knowing you would have over 200 individual conversations telling each employee, one by one, that he or she would no longer be an employee of the company. It would have been much easier to send out pink slips or to ask other managers to deliver the news. This CEO decided, however, to take on the task himself. Even though he was delivering bad news, his courage as a CEO coupled with his empathy in his communication massively raised his credibility as a leader.

 Learning the Lesson:
Being a strong leader doesn't mean you have to be stone cold or hide your sensitive side from colleagues and team members. Team members not only want to see an action-oriented, convicted leader, they want to see their leader as a human being capable of caring for her team members. They want to see that when a leader needs to make a difficult decision, such as an employee layoff, she takes pains in making those decisions and considers how they affect people. Team members don't want to see a leader who makes difficult decisions which adversely affect people with indifference or, even worse, with glee.

So why do team members want to see the human side of a leader at a time when she must make difficult people decisions? Two key reasons come to mind. First, team members want to know that the leader values other humans and doesn't view them as just numbers on a spreadsheet or boxes on an organization chart. The second reason is that team members want to know that a leader doesn't take difficult people decisions lightly and has done his or her due-diligence in evaluating the decision alternatives. Team members understand that leaders sometimes need to make tough people decisions; they also want to know that the leader didn't take the decision lightly.

Why do some leaders have difficulty with empathy? Several reasons abound:

- **Empathy is viewed as a sign of weakness –** Some leaders see showing empathy as a lack of courage. Under this viewpoint, the unempathetic leader can make decisions driven by the best interest of the organization rather than a namby-pamby decision made in fear of hurting someone's feelings.

- **Tough people decisions are easier when the leader can mentally take people out of the equation –** Rather than risk showing too much empathy and becoming emotionally enslaved to the decision, some leaders throw up the shields and don't show any empathy at all. The decision becomes one of numbers, not people.

- **The leader is making a questionable decision –** Showing transparency and empathy in a decision requires the leader to demonstrate sound logic. If the leader is making a poor decision based on something other than sound business thinking, showing empathy may reveal that the decision is questionable.

Adding it up:
Empathetic leaders are still able to make sound business decisions; they just allow themselves to feel for the human beings they work with. Being an empathetic leader means putting the following pieces in place:

- **Put yourself in the recipient's shoes –** When you're preparing for a difficult discussion, truly turn the tables and pretend the message is being delivered to you. It also may help to have a trusted colleague or coach role-play a discussion with you. After you've done your table-turn or role-play, do an honest assessment of how it went. If your messaging is coming across as cold or ruthless, then revise the messaging to raise the empathy curve.

- **Be direct with respect –** Now is not the time for vagueness, disrespectful behavior, or excuses. If you've got a tough message to deliver, deliver it as succinctly and respectfully as possible. It's already a difficult situation; don't make it even more difficult by mucking up the soup with inappropriate communication.

- **Explain the "why"** – When you explain the "why" behind a communication, you demonstrate respect for the recipient by showing the logic of your thinking. For example, rather than saying, "We will no longer reimburse employees for business-class travel on flights," consider saying, "Travel costs are up 40 percent over last year which means we need to look for ways to save money on travel to keep from cutting other vital programs. One way to do this is to require everyone to fly coach-class on all flights." Team members may not like the answer any better, but they will respect that you are using and communicating sound logic.

Graduating with honors:
We're human. We have the ability to express an identical statement many ways depending on our mood, emotions, and intentions. Team members want to know that while you make sound, intelligent decisions, you also lead with your *heart* and care about the people you lead. If you've found yourself in a mode where you view people as numbers on a spreadsheet, get up out of your chair and go talk to your team members. Showing empathy and interest in your team members will give you a reputation as a leader who cares, as opposed to a ruthless tyrant.

Why Don't They Follow Me?

I hope you've enjoyed **Why Don't They Follow Me?** as much as I enjoyed writing it. My desire is that you found a few nuggets which you can put into your leadership arsenal and improve your leadership skills.

Let me leave you with a few closing thoughts:

- Don't read this once and put it on a shelf, never to see light again. Refer back to it occasionally to help you re-ground your leadership skills and get back to basics.

- If you've got a lot of things to work on, don't try to do it all at once. Take no more than three things at a time; don't overwhelm yourself with too many things to do.

- Make frequent use of coaches or mentors. To this day I still use coaches to help me when writing books, articles, or seminars. Having someone tell you that you are moving in the right direction (or that you're way out in left field) is very valuable and something that you'll never outgrow.

- Remember to have fun and laugh along the way. Leadership is tough stuff, but it's not something that should wreck your life or you should stress about. Relax and treat your leadership journey as a never-ending lesson.

More Books by Lonnie Pacelli

The Project Management Advisor: 18 Major Project Screw-Ups and How to Cut Them Off at the Pass (Prentice Hall, 2004)

The Truth About Getting Your Point Across...And Nothing But the Truth (Prentice Hall, 2006)

The Leadership Made Simple Series (Amazon.com, e-book only,2006)

Six-Word Lessons for Project Managers (Pacelli Publishing, 2009)

Six-Word Lessons for Dads with Autistic Kids (Pacelli Publishing, 2013)

All books are available in print and e-book on Amazon, kindle, iTunes, Nook and more.

To learn more about all of Lonnie's books, blog, articles and publications, visit **LonniePacelli.com**.

Why Don't They Follow Me?

The *Six-Word Lessons Series,* founded by Lonnie Pacelli

Legend has it that Ernest Hemingway was challenged to write a story using only six words. He responded with the story, "For sale: baby shoes, never worn." The story tickles the imagination. Why were the shoes never worn? The answers are left up to the reader's imagination.

This style of writing has a number of aliases: postcard fiction, flash fiction, and micro fiction. Lonnie Pacelli was introduced to this concept in 2009 by a friend, and started thinking about how this extreme brevity could apply to today's communication culture of text messages, tweets and Facebook posts. He wrote the first book, *Six-Word Lessons for Project Managers*, then started helping other authors write and publish their own books in the series.

Each book has about ten six-word chapters with 100 six-word lesson titles, each followed by a one-page description. They can be written by entrepreneurs who want to promote their businesses, or anyone with a message to share. Learn how to write your own book at **6wordlessons.com.**

Why Don't They Follow Me?

Why Don't They Follow Me?